Trailblazing Women

Stories of Courage, Resilience, and Triumph

By Elena Sinclair

2

Contents

Trailblazing Women: Stories of Courage, Resilience, and Triumph...5

Chapter 1. Pioneering in Science............................ 12

Chapter 2. Breaking Barriers in the Art 21

Chapter 3. Triumphs in Politics and Activism 29

Chapter 4. Trailblazing in Business and Entrepreneurship.. 37

Chapter 5. Defying Odds in Sports......................... 45

Chapter 6. Struggles and Triumphs in Education 53

Chapter 7. Overcoming Adversity in Medicine............... 62

Chapter 8. Defending Human Rights 72

Chapter 9. Innovators in Technology................................. 82

Chapter 10. Legacy and Future Trailblazers.................... 91

Navigating the Trial of Triumph......................... 100

COPYRIGHT © 2024 ELENA SINCLAIR
All Rights Reserved.

Trailblazing Women: Stories of Courage, Resilience, and Triumph

Welcome to a journey of inspiration, courage, and triumph as we embark on an exploration of the lives of extraordinary women who have left an indelible mark on the canvas of history. "Trailblazing Women: Stories of Courage, Resilience, and Triumph" is more than just a collection of tales; it's a celebration of the incredible women who defied societal norms, shattered glass ceilings, and blazed trails across various fields.

Picture this: a world where women are celebrated for their achievements, where their stories are woven into the very fabric of our collective narrative. That's the world we envision as we dive into the pages of this book—a world where the courage of women is recognized, their resilience admired, and their triumphs celebrated.

The Genesis of Trailblazing Women

Why this book, you might wonder? Well, the answer lies in the countless stories of remarkable women who, more often than not, find themselves relegated to the margins of history. It's time to bring these stories into the spotlight, to shine a bright light on the women who challenged the status quo, overcame obstacles, and paved the way for generations to come.

As we set out on this literary adventure, imagine sitting down for a chat with each of these trailblazing women over a cup of coffee or tea. Picture the laughter, the shared struggles, and the wisdom exchanged in these intimate conversations. That's the spirit we aim to capture—a friendly, engaging, and empowering conversation that transcends the pages of this book.

A Tapestry of Courage

The heart of this collection lies in the courage that beats within the stories of these women. We delve into the realms of science, arts, politics, business, sports, education, medicine, technology, and human rights. In each chapter, we encounter a fearless woman who faced challenges head-on, armed with determination and an unwavering belief in her abilities.

From the laboratories of scientific discovery to the corridors of political power, from the hallowed halls of academia to the adrenaline-pumping arenas of sports, these women have been there, done that, and rewritten the rulebook while at it. Their stories are not just tales of personal triumph but blueprints for breaking barriers and forging paths where there were none.

An Invitation to Explore

Consider this book your personal invitation to explore the untold stories of women who dared to dream, challenged the norm, and emerged victorious. Each turn of the page reveals a new adventure, a fresh perspective, and a deeper understanding of the resilience that resides within the hearts of these remarkable women.

As you read, you'll find yourself transported into the shoes of a pioneering scientist, a revolutionary artist, a tenacious politician, a visionary entrepreneur, an unstoppable athlete, a dedicated educator, a compassionate healthcare professional, a tireless advocate for human rights, and an innovative tech trailblazer. Through their eyes, you'll witness the world as they saw it—a world full of challenges waiting to be turned into opportunities.

A Celebration of Diversity

One of the most beautiful aspects of this collection is the diversity it encapsulates. The women featured here come from different corners of the globe, diverse backgrounds, and varied walks of life. Their stories unfold against backdrops as varied as the colors of a rainbow, illustrating that courage, resilience, and triumph know no boundaries.

From the bustling streets of urban metropolises to the quiet corners of rural landscapes, these women have navigated a myriad of challenges. In doing so, they've not only shaped their individual destinies but also left an enduring impact on the communities and societies they've touched.

Friendship in the Margins

In the margins of history, where the stories of these women often find themselves, there exists a quiet camaraderie—a friendship among women who, separated by time and space, share a common journey. This book is a celebration of that friendship. It's an acknowledgment that the struggles faced by one woman echo in the challenges overcome by another.

As you read about these trailblazing women, consider yourself a welcomed friend, a confidante privy to the joys, sorrows, victories, and defeats that make up the fabric of their lives. It's a testament to the power of storytelling, connecting us across generations and continents.

Looking Forward

As we navigate the pages of "Trailblazing Women," let's not merely marvel at the achievements of the past but also look forward to the future. The stories within these chapters are not relics of bygone eras; they are beacons guiding us toward a more inclusive, equitable, and compassionate world.

Let these tales inspire conversations, spark new ideas, and kindle the flame of determination within you. May the courage, resilience, and triumphs of these women serve as a reminder that, regardless of who you are or where you come from, your story matters, and you have the power to shape the narrative of tomorrow.

Conclusion: A Shared Journey

As we conclude this introduction, know that you are not alone in this journey. The women whose stories you are about to discover have walked similar paths, faced similar challenges, and emerged with heads held high. So, grab a cozy blanket, your favorite beverage, and immerse yourself in the vibrant stories of Trailblazing Women. Here's to the courage to dream, the resilience to overcome, and the triumphs that await on the horizon. Cheers to the incredible women who inspire us all!

CHAPTER 1. PIONEERING IN SCIENCE

In this corner of our journey through "Trailblazing Women: Stories of Courage, Resilience, and Triumph," we're delving into the stories of women who not only navigated the intricate web of scientific discovery but also broke through the gender barriers of their time. These are the women whose curiosity knew no bounds, whose passion for knowledge transcended societal expectations, and whose groundbreaking contributions have left an indelible mark on the world of science.

The Early Days of Exploration

Our journey begins with the pioneers, those intrepid women who dared to explore the unknown territories of scientific discovery when the landscape was predominantly male-dominated. Imagine a time when the scientific community was a fortress with high walls, and women were often kept outside the gates. Yet, amidst this challenging terrain, our trailblazing women donned their metaphorical lab coats, picked up their metaphorical magnifying glasses, and stepped onto the scientific stage.

One such woman, let's call her Dr. Pioneer, comes to the forefront. Dr. Pioneer's story is a testament to the resilience required to traverse uncharted territories. Born in an era when women were expected to limit their aspirations to domestic spheres, Dr. Pioneer harbored a burning curiosity for the mysteries of the natural world. Her journey started with a humble fascination for the stars, microbes, or the unseen forces shaping our existence.

Breaking the Glass Ceiling

Dr. Pioneer's path was not paved with rose petals. The glass ceiling above her was as thick as it was transparent. Yet, armed with determination and an unyielding passion for science, she began chipping away at that ceiling, bit by bit. Each experiment, each discovery, and each paper published was a crack in the glass, letting in the light of possibility for those who would follow.

Our friendly scientist faced skepticism, raised eyebrows, and doors closed because of her gender. However, she persisted. She joined laboratories where men outnumbered women tenfold, and she proved that scientific prowess knows no gender. Her journey was not only about advancing knowledge but also about dismantling the stereotypes that restricted women's involvement in the scientific enterprise.

Groundbreaking Discoveries

As we turn the pages of Dr. Pioneer's life, we witness her making groundbreaking discoveries that reshaped the scientific landscape. Perhaps she unlocked the secrets of the cosmos, revealing the mysteries of distant galaxies. Or, she might have delved into the microscopic realm, uncovering the hidden intricacies of life at the cellular level. Whatever the field, her contributions were not just significant but transformative.

Imagine the thrill of standing at the precipice of a scientific breakthrough, the exhilaration of connecting the dots that no one else saw. Dr. Pioneer's triumphs were not just personal victories; they were victories for science, for women, and for the collective understanding of the world.

Navigating Challenges with Grace

Yet, the journey was far from a stroll in the park. Dr. Pioneer faced challenges that tested not only her intellect but also her resilience. The scrutiny she endured, the prejudices she faced, and the extra hurdles placed in her path were not trivial. However, she met these challenges with grace, turning adversity into fuel for her determination.

Perhaps she found solace in the camaraderie of like-minded colleagues, forming alliances that transcended gender. Or, she might have sought refuge in the joy of discovery, finding fulfillment in the pursuit of knowledge that goes beyond societal expectations. Dr. Pioneer's story is not just about scientific achievement but also about the human spirit's capacity to triumph over adversity.

Legacy in Education and Mentorship

As we delve deeper into Dr. Pioneer's narrative, we uncover another layer of her legacy—a commitment to education and mentorship. Recognizing the importance of paving the way for future generations, she became a mentor, guiding aspiring scientists, especially women, through the labyrinth of academia and research.

Dr. Pioneer's classrooms echoed with encouragement, her laboratories became havens of inclusion, and her mentorship programs opened doors for those who had been historically marginalized. Her dedication to education extended beyond the textbooks; it was about fostering an environment where anyone with a passion for science, regardless of gender, could thrive.

The Ripple Effect

Dr. Pioneer's impact didn't stop within the walls of laboratories or lecture halls. Her contributions created a ripple effect, influencing policies, norms, and perceptions within the scientific community. She became a symbol of possibility, a living testament to the idea that anyone, regardless of gender, could contribute significantly to the advancement of knowledge.

The women who followed in her footsteps found a more welcoming scientific landscape, thanks to the cracks she had created in the glass ceiling. Dr. Pioneer's story became not just a personal triumph but a beacon of hope for those who aspired to tread the scientific path.

Celebrating the Whole Scientist

In the friendly and inclusive spirit of our exploration, it's crucial to celebrate not just Dr. Pioneer's scientific achievements but the multifaceted nature of her identity. She was not only a scientist but a friend, a family member, and a member of a broader community. Her story reminds us that behind every groundbreaking discovery is a person with passions, dreams, and a life beyond the laboratory.

Her friendly demeanor, approachability, and willingness to share the wonders of science with others created an atmosphere where learning and discovery thrived. Dr. Pioneer embodied the idea that being a scientist didn't require sacrificing one's humanity; instead, it enhanced it.

A Call to Action

As we conclude our exploration of Chapter 1, we find ourselves not just inspired by Dr. Pioneer's scientific achievements but also compelled to action. Her story challenges us to question and dismantle the barriers that still exist for women in science today. It calls for a collective effort to create an environment where every aspiring scientist, regardless of gender, can flourish.

Let Dr. Pioneer's journey be a catalyst for change—a reminder that the pursuit of knowledge is a collective endeavor, and the scientific community is richer when diverse voices and perspectives are embraced. As we celebrate the strides made by women in science, let us also recognize the work that remains, ensuring that future chapters in the book of scientific discovery are written with an even more inclusive and diverse cast of characters.

So, here's to Dr. Pioneer and to all the women who paved the way, who questioned the norms, and who continue to inspire us to reach for the stars, whether metaphorical or celestial. As we turn the page to our next chapter, we carry with us the warmth of Dr. Pioneer's friendly spirit and the excitement of discovery that propels us ever forward into the unexplored territories of knowledge.

Chapter 2. Breaking Barriers in the Art

In this vibrant chapter, we step into the world of artistic expression, where women have not only carved their names but also shattered the barriers that sought to confine their creativity. Join us as we explore the lives of women who dared to redefine artistic norms, challenge conventions, and leave an indelible mark on the world of arts.

Unveiling the Canvas

Imagine a world where artistic spaces were confined by the brushstrokes of tradition, where the canvases were dominated by a palette dictated by societal norms. Yet, amid this seemingly restrictive landscape, enter our fearless artist, whom we affectionately call Maestro Muse. She's a visionary who doesn't just paint or sculpt; she crafts stories, emotions, and revolutions with every stroke and chisel.

Maestro Muse's journey into the arts wasn't a mere pursuit of a hobby—it was a rebellion. Born in an era when the arts were considered a male stronghold, she picked up her tools of expression and set out to challenge the notion that creativity had a gender.

The Symphony of Resilience

Maestro Muse faced challenges that echoed through the hallowed halls of art institutions. Her very presence was often met with raised eyebrows and skepticism. Society, entrenched in its biases, questioned whether a woman could wield a paintbrush with the same mastery as her male counterparts. However, undeterred, she turned every challenge into an opportunity to showcase her resilience.

In the spirit of friendly conversation, let's imagine sitting down with Maestro Muse over a cup of coffee or tea. In her warm and inviting studio, surrounded by the colors of her imagination, she shares stories of overcoming doubts, defying expectations, and finding strength in her passion for the arts. Her journey becomes not just a narrative of personal triumph but a symphony of resilience that resonates with every aspiring artist.

Challenging Artistic Norms

Maestro Muse's art wasn't just about creating aesthetically pleasing compositions; it was a rebellion against the status quo. Perhaps she dabbled in abstract expressionism when realism dominated the scene, or she embraced unconventional mediums to challenge the traditional boundaries of art. Her creations were not just brushstrokes on canvas; they were statements challenging the very definition of what could be considered art.

In our friendly chat with Maestro Muse, she might reveal the stories behind her most controversial pieces—the ones that sparked conversations, raised eyebrows, and ultimately expanded the horizons of artistic expression. Her journey encourages us to question the norms that define art, to embrace the unconventional, and to recognize that creativity knows no boundaries.

Empowering Through Art

One of the most inspiring aspects of Maestro Muse's story lies in her commitment to empower others through art. She recognized the transformative power of artistic expression and sought to make it accessible to everyone, irrespective of their background or gender. Maestro Muse transformed her studio into a welcoming space, inviting aspiring artists, especially women, to explore their creative potential.

In our friendly conversation, she might share anecdotes of mentoring emerging talents, breaking down the barriers that hindered their artistic journeys. Her commitment to fostering a community of artists speaks not only to her artistic prowess but also to her understanding of the arts as a tool for empowerment and social change.

Redefining Beauty and Representation

Maestro Muse's canvas wasn't just a space for personal expression; it became a platform for redefining beauty and representation. In an art world where the standards of beauty were often narrow and exclusive, she challenged the norms by celebrating diversity in her creations. Her paintings and sculptures became mirrors reflecting the rich tapestry of humanity, where every stroke conveyed a message of inclusivity.

As we sip our drinks in Maestro Muse's studio, we might discuss the evolution of her artistic vision—how she consciously chose subjects that defied societal beauty standards, how she highlighted the beauty in imperfections, and how she challenged the notion that art should conform to a predetermined mold. Her story becomes a celebration of art as a vehicle for changing perceptions and fostering a more inclusive society.

The Impact Beyond the Canvas

Maestro Muse's influence didn't confine itself to the walls of galleries or the pages of art history books. Her impact rippled through communities, sparking conversations about the role of women in the arts, the power of creativity in social change, and the need for diverse voices in artistic expression.

In our friendly dialogue with Maestro Muse, she might recount instances of art installations that transformed public spaces, of community projects that brought people together through shared artistic experiences, and of the joy that comes from witnessing the transformative power of art beyond the studio. Her story encourages us to view art not just as a personal expression but as a catalyst for societal transformation.

Celebrating the Whole Artist

In the spirit of our friendly exploration, it's essential to celebrate not just Maestro Muse's artistic achievements but also the multidimensional nature of her identity. She wasn't just an artist; she was a friend, a storyteller, and a cultural influencer. Her story reminds us that behind every masterpiece is a person with dreams, challenges, and a life beyond the canvas.

Our chat with Maestro Muse would likely touch on her inspirations, her creative process, and the moments of vulnerability that are inherent in the artistic journey. Her friendly demeanor and willingness to share not just her art but also the stories woven into each piece create an atmosphere where art becomes a conversation, a dialogue between the artist and the audience.

A Call to Embrace Artistic Diversity

As we conclude our exploration of Chapter 2, let's carry with us the vibrancy of Maestro Muse's artistic spirit and the lessons embedded in her journey. Her story calls us to embrace artistic diversity, to challenge preconceived notions, and to recognize the power of creativity in reshaping the narrative of our collective culture.

Maestro Muse's legacy invites us to actively seek out and celebrate the work of artists from diverse backgrounds, to create spaces where different voices and perspectives can flourish, and to view art not as a singular expression but as a mosaic that reflects the rich diversity of the human experience.

So, here's to Maestro Muse and to all the women who dared to break barriers in the arts. As we turn the page to our next chapter, let's carry the warmth of artistic expression in our hearts and the understanding that, just like Maestro Muse, each of us has the power to add our unique colors to the canvas of the world.

CHAPTER 3. TRIUMPHS IN POLITICS AND ACTIVISM

In this captivating chapter, we dive into the realms of politics and activism, where women have not only entered the arena but have triumphed against the currents of societal expectations. Join us as we explore the inspiring stories of women who navigated the complex landscape of politics and activism, leaving an enduring legacy of courage and change.

Setting the Stage

Imagine a political landscape dominated by men, where the corridors of power echoed with the voices of the privileged few. Yet, into this arena strides our fearless protagonist, Advocate Athena, a woman who wasn't content to remain on the sidelines. In our friendly exploration, let's envision sitting down with Advocate Athena over a cup of coffee or tea, as she shares the tales of her journey into the heart of politics and activism.

Breaking the Political Mold

Advocate Athena's journey wasn't a conventional one. Born in an era when women were often relegated to supporting roles in political spheres, she defied expectations and aimed for the very heart of governance. Whether she entered local politics, national governance, or international diplomacy, her story is one of breaking through the barriers that sought to confine her to the periphery.

In our friendly chat, Advocate Athena might share anecdotes of the skepticism she faced, the doors that were initially closed to her, and the resilience she summoned to not only open those doors but also to redefine the political narrative. Her journey becomes a testament to the idea that politics is not a gendered arena—it's a space for those with the passion and vision to enact positive change.

Championing Social Justice

Advocate Athena's foray into politics wasn't merely about acquiring power; it was about wielding that power to champion social justice causes. Picture her as a voice for the voiceless, a tireless advocate for marginalized communities, and a force for change within legislative chambers. In our friendly conversation, she might recount the battles fought and won on behalf of those who needed a champion in the political arena.

Her triumphs become a source of inspiration, not just for aspiring politicians but for anyone who believes in the power of policy and governance to address societal inequalities. Advocate Athena's story underscores the idea that political power, when harnessed with integrity and empathy, becomes a tool for transformation.

Navigating the Political Landscape

As we chat with Advocate Athena, we delve into the nuances of navigating the political landscape. Perhaps she formed alliances with like-minded colleagues, transcending party lines in pursuit of common goals. Maybe she faced opposition that questioned her right to be in the political arena, or she encountered challenges that tested her resolve. Her friendly demeanor might reveal the strategies she employed to bridge divides, build consensus, and enact meaningful change.

In our exploration, we come to understand that politics is not a solitary endeavor but a collaborative effort. Advocate Athena's ability to navigate the political landscape becomes a valuable lesson in diplomacy, resilience, and the art of compromise for the greater good.

Activism Beyond Rhetoric

Advocate Athena's journey extends beyond the political chambers into the realm of activism. In our friendly conversation, she might share stories of rallies, protests, and movements she spearheaded or joined in the pursuit of social change. Her activism isn't confined to grand gestures; it's rooted in the belief that collective action, no matter how small, can drive systemic change.

The streets become her platform, the placards her voice, and the collective energy of activists her driving force. As we explore Advocate Athena's activism, we recognize that politics and activism are intertwined, each reinforcing the other in the pursuit of a more just and equitable society.

Legacy in Mentorship and Education

Advocate Athena's story takes a poignant turn as we uncover her commitment to mentorship and education. Recognizing the importance of passing the torch to the next generation, she becomes a guiding light for aspiring politicians and activists. In our friendly chat, she might share anecdotes of mentorship programs, political education initiatives, and the joy she finds in empowering the leaders of tomorrow.

Her legacy extends not just through the policies she championed but through the individuals she inspired. In our exploration, we discover that Advocate Athena's impact isn't measured solely in legislative victories but also in the minds and hearts of those who continue her work.

Challenges as Catalysts for Change

No political journey is without its challenges, and Advocate Athena's story is no exception. Perhaps she faced discrimination based on her gender, received backlash for her progressive stances, or encountered resistance from entrenched interests. In our friendly dialogue, she might share how these challenges, instead of deterring her, became catalysts for even greater determination.

Advocate Athena's ability to turn adversity into fuel for change becomes a source of inspiration for us all. Her story reminds us that challenges are not roadblocks but opportunities to redefine the narrative and push for the changes we believe in.

A Call to Engage

As we conclude our exploration of Chapter 3, Advocate Athena's story calls us to engage with the political and activist spheres in our own ways. Whether it's running for office, joining a grassroots movement, or actively participating in civic initiatives, her journey inspires us to recognize our agency in shaping the societies we want to live in.

Advocate Athena's legacy encourages us not to view politics and activism as distant realms but as spaces where our voices matter. Her story becomes a friendly nudge, inviting us to actively participate in the democratic process, contribute to social justice causes, and engage in the conversations that shape the world around us.

So, here's to Advocate Athena and to all the women who triumphed in politics and activism. As we turn the page to our next chapter, let's carry the spirit of active engagement, the belief that positive change is possible, and the understanding that, in the friendly dialogue of democracy, every voice counts.

Chapter 4. Trailblazing in Business and Entrepreneurship

Welcome to Chapter 4 of our odyssey through "Trailblazing Women: Stories of Courage, Resilience, and Triumph." This chapter invites us into the dynamic world of business and entrepreneurship, where women have not only shattered glass ceilings but also built empires from the shards. Join us as we embark on a friendly exploration of the tales of women who dared to dream, disrupt, and redefine success in the business landscape.

The Entrepreneurial Frontier

Picture this: a landscape dominated by corporate giants, where boardrooms echo with the voices of a predominantly male executive class. Yet, in this terrain, our protagonist, whom we affectionately call Visionary Venture, emerges as a trailblazer. In our friendly conversation, let's imagine sitting down with Visionary Venture over a cup of coffee or tea, as she shares the stories of her entrepreneurial journey.

Dismantling Corporate Norms

Visionary Venture's journey wasn't one of conformity; it was a conscious effort to dismantle corporate norms that limited the aspirations of women. Born in an era when the business world was often deemed inaccessible to female leaders, she embarked on a path that not only challenged the status quo but also redefined what success in business could look like.

In our friendly chat, Visionary Venture might recount the early days when she faced skepticism and naysayers who questioned her ability to navigate the complexities of business. Yet, armed with a vision, determination, and a knack for innovation, she transformed doubts into fuel for her entrepreneurial fire.

Building Empires

The heart of Visionary Venture's story lies in her ability to not just compete but to build empires from the ground up. Whether she ventured into tech, fashion, finance, or any other industry, her approach was characterized by boldness, innovation, and an unwavering belief in her capabilities.

As we chat, we might hear anecdotes of the risks she took, the challenges she overcame, and the triumphs that followed. Visionary Venture's story becomes a beacon for aspiring entrepreneurs, illustrating that success is not confined to a specific gender but is the result of vision, hard work, and resilience.

Innovating for Change

Our friendly exploration takes us deeper into Visionary Venture's entrepreneurial philosophy—an unyielding commitment to innovation. Perhaps she introduced groundbreaking products, disrupted traditional business models, or embraced sustainability before it became a buzzword. Her story is not just about financial success but about the transformative power of innovation in driving positive change.

In our conversation, we might discover how Visionary Venture's innovations were not solely driven by profit motives but were rooted in a broader vision for societal impact. Her journey becomes a reminder that entrepreneurship, when coupled with a sense of responsibility, has the potential to address pressing issues and contribute to the betterment of communities.

Cultivating Inclusive Workplaces

One of the distinctive threads in Visionary Venture's narrative is her commitment to cultivating inclusive workplaces. In our friendly dialogue, she might share stories of fostering diversity, equity, and inclusion within her organizations. Her approach recognizes the value of diverse perspectives and underscores that the success of a business is intricately linked to the diversity of its workforce.

Visionary Venture's story becomes not just a guide for aspiring entrepreneurs but also a call to action for creating workplaces where everyone, regardless of gender or background, can thrive. In our exploration, we discover that her commitment to inclusivity goes beyond mere rhetoric—it's ingrained in the very fabric of her entrepreneurial journey.

Balancing Leadership and Empathy

As we delve into the chapters of Visionary Venture's life, we encounter a harmonious balance between leadership and empathy. In our friendly chat, she might share insights into how she led with decisiveness while also fostering a workplace culture that valued the well-being and growth of her team.

Visionary Venture's story challenges the notion that leadership requires sacrificing empathy or that success comes at the expense of human connection. Her journey becomes a friendly reminder that businesses can be both profitable and compassionate, and that a leader's strength lies not just in strategy but in the ability to inspire and uplift those around them.

Navigating Challenges with Grace

Entrepreneurship is a journey marked by challenges, and Visionary Venture's story is no exception. In our friendly conversation, she might open up about the setbacks, the moments of self-doubt, and the times when the entrepreneurial path seemed like an uphill climb. However, her ability to navigate challenges with grace, to learn from failures, and to persist in the face of adversity becomes an inspiring narrative for anyone charting their course in the business world.

Visionary Venture's story is not about the absence of challenges but about the resilience to overcome them. In our exploration, we discover that the entrepreneurial journey is as much about the setbacks as it is about the triumphs, and that every stumbling block is an opportunity for growth.

Legacy in Mentorship and Giving Back

As Visionary Venture's tale unfolds, we encounter a significant chapter—the legacy she leaves through mentorship and giving back. In our friendly chat, she might share stories of mentoring aspiring entrepreneurs, supporting initiatives for women in business, or investing in programs that nurture the next generation of leaders.

Her commitment to mentorship becomes a testament to the belief that success is most meaningful when shared. Visionary Venture's story is not just about individual triumphs but about creating a ripple effect of positive impact that extends far beyond the boardroom.

A Call to Entrepreneurial Action

As we conclude our exploration of Chapter 4, Visionary Venture's story extends a friendly call to entrepreneurial action. Her journey inspires us to dream boldly, innovate fearlessly, and lead with empathy. Whether we are seasoned entrepreneurs or aspiring trailblazers, her story becomes a guidebook for navigating the entrepreneurial landscape with purpose and resilience.

Visionary Venture's legacy encourages us to view business not merely as a vehicle for financial success but as a platform for positive change. As we turn the page to our next chapter, let's carry with us the entrepreneurial spirit of Visionary Venture—the belief that, in the friendly dialogue of business, every venture is an opportunity to make a difference.

44

CHAPTER 5. DEFYING ODDS IN SPORTS

This chapter unfolds on the vibrant fields, courts, and arenas of sports—a realm often dominated by male prowess. Yet, here, in this chapter, we celebrate the indomitable spirit of women athletes who not only stepped onto the playing field but also defied the odds, leaving an inspiring legacy of triumph. Join us as we embark on a friendly exploration of the stories of women who conquered challenges, shattered stereotypes, and proved that the game belongs to all.

The Playing Field as an Equalizer

Imagine a world where sports were seen as a male domain, where stadiums echoed with cheers for male athletes, and where women were often relegated to the sidelines. Now, envision our central character, whom we affectionately call Fearless Fielder, stepping onto the playing field with determination in her eyes and a love for the game in her heart.

In our friendly chat with Fearless Fielder, we explore the early days when she first picked up a ball, racket, or any other sporting equipment. Her journey wasn't just about mastering the skills of the game; it was a rebellion against the notion that certain sports were off-limits to women. She became a symbol of the idea that the playing field is an equalizer—a space where talent, skill, and passion know no gender.

Shattering Stereotypes in Sports

Fearless Fielder's story unfolds not just in victories but in the courage to challenge stereotypes deeply ingrained in the world of sports. In our friendly conversation, we might hear about the raised eyebrows when she joined the team, the assumptions she defied, and the resilience she displayed in proving that athleticism knows no gender.

Whether she conquered the basketball court, dominated the soccer field, or set records in the swimming pool, Fearless Fielder's journey becomes a testament to the power of breaking down barriers. She didn't just play the game; she changed the rules and, in doing so, paved the way for future generations of women athletes.

Overcoming Adversity

Sports, by nature, are a terrain of challenges—physical, mental, and often societal. In our friendly dialogue with Fearless Fielder, we explore the moments when the odds seemed stacked against her. Perhaps it was recovering from an injury, facing discrimination, or dealing with the pressure to conform to conventional notions of femininity.

Her triumphs over adversity become stories of resilience, determination, and the unyielding belief that challenges are stepping stones to success. Fearless Fielder's journey teaches us that setbacks are not the end of the game but opportunities to come back stronger, smarter, and more determined.

Trailblazing in Uncharted Territories

Fearless Fielder's impact extends beyond the playing field. In our friendly chat, she might share stories of entering sports where women were traditionally underrepresented—whether it be in extreme sports, combat sports, or any other arena where female athletes were a rarity.

Her foray into uncharted territories becomes a celebration of courage and a reminder that women can excel in any sport they choose. Fearless Fielder's story inspires a generation of girls to see themselves as potential trailblazers, proving that the boundaries of sports are continually expanding, thanks to the courage of athletes like her.

Fostering a Culture of Inclusivity

Fearless Fielder's journey is not just about personal triumphs; it's about fostering a culture of inclusivity in the world of sports. In our friendly conversation, she might share how she actively worked to create environments where aspiring female athletes felt welcomed, supported, and encouraged to pursue their sporting dreams.

Her commitment to inclusivity is not a mere slogan but a lived experience. Fearless Fielder's story becomes a catalyst for change within sports organizations, encouraging them to reevaluate policies, challenge biases, and actively work toward creating a level playing field for athletes of all genders.

Breaking Records and Redefining Excellence

Our exploration with Fearless Fielder naturally leads us to the moments when she not only competed but set records and redefined what excellence in sports means. Whether she achieved a milestone in scoring, broke speed records, or showcased unmatched skill, her story becomes a source of inspiration for athletes aiming not just to participate but to excel at the highest levels.

In our friendly dialogue, we might delve into the strategies she employed, the dedication she exhibited, and the joy she found in pushing the boundaries of what was deemed possible. Fearless Fielder's journey is a friendly nudge for athletes to dream big, work hard, and challenge themselves to reach new heights.

Legacy in Sportsmanship and Mentorship

As we progress through Fearless Fielder's narrative, we encounter a pivotal chapter—her legacy in sportsmanship and mentorship. In our friendly chat, she might share stories of the camaraderie she fostered with teammates, the respect she showed opponents, and the joy she found in the essence of sports—the spirit of fair play and mutual respect.

Her commitment to mentorship becomes a powerful force for change. Fearless Fielder actively engages in nurturing the next generation of athletes, sharing her experiences, providing guidance, and instilling in them the values of sportsmanship. Her legacy is not just in the records she set but in the impact she leaves on the character and ethos of the sporting community.

A Call to Athletic Empowerment

As we wrap up our exploration of Chapter 5, Fearless Fielder's story extends a friendly call to athletic empowerment. Her journey challenges us to rethink the narratives surrounding women in sports, to actively support inclusivity, and to recognize that the field of play belongs to all who have the passion and the drive to excel.

Fearless Fielder's legacy encourages athletes to be more than competitors—to be advocates for change, mentors to those who follow, and ambassadors for the true spirit of sportsmanship. As we turn the page to our next chapter, let's carry with us the inspiration of Fearless Fielder, the belief that the playing field is a space for everyone, and the understanding that, in the world of sports, triumph is not just about winning games but about overcoming the odds with grace and determination.

Chapter 6. Struggles and Triumphs in Education

In this chapter, we delve into the world of education—a realm where women have faced challenges, broken barriers, and triumphed in their pursuit of knowledge and academic excellence. Join us in this friendly exploration of the stories of women who, against societal norms, navigated the educational landscape, leaving an indelible mark on the pursuit of learning.

The Educational Odyssey Begins

Let's imagine our central character, whom we affectionately call Scholarly Trailblazer, stepping onto the educational stage. In our friendly conversation with Scholarly Trailblazer, we uncover the early days of her educational journey. Born in an era when educational opportunities for women were often limited, she embarked on a quest for knowledge that would defy expectations and reshape the narrative of women's role in academia.

Scholarly Trailblazer's journey was not just about attending classes and earning degrees; it was a conscious decision to challenge the norms that dictated women's educational paths. In our friendly chat, she might share anecdotes of the raised eyebrows, the skepticism, and the resilience required to pave the way for future generations of women in academia.

Breaking Educational Barriers

As we delve deeper into Scholarly Trailblazer's story, we encounter the barriers she had to break through. Whether it was gaining admission to prestigious institutions, accessing courses traditionally reserved for men, or pursuing advanced degrees, her journey becomes a testament to the tenacity required to break educational barriers.

In our exploration, we might discover the pivotal moments when Scholarly Trailblazer faced doors slammed shut and ceilings that seemed impenetrable. Yet, armed with an unyielding passion for learning, she shattered those barriers, not just for herself but for those who would follow in her academic footsteps.

A Struggle for Recognition

Scholarly Trailblazer's story unfolds against the backdrop of a struggle for recognition. In an academic landscape where women's contributions were often overlooked, she fought not only for her rightful place but also to have her ideas, research, and achievements acknowledged on equal footing with her male counterparts.

In our friendly chat, Scholarly Trailblazer might recount instances of having to work twice as hard to earn the same recognition, of facing biases that questioned her intellectual capabilities, and of the determination that fueled her pursuit of excellence. Her journey becomes a narrative of not just academic accomplishment but a triumph over the societal norms that sought to diminish women's contributions in the realm of ideas.

Pioneering in Fields of Study

Our exploration takes us to Scholarly Trailblazer's choice of fields of study—a realm where women were often scarce. Whether it was in the sciences, humanities, or any other discipline, she dared to enter uncharted territories. In our friendly conversation, we might uncover the stories behind her decision to pursue a particular field, the challenges she faced in male-dominated classrooms, and the groundbreaking contributions she made to her chosen discipline.

Scholarly Trailblazer's pioneering spirit becomes a source of inspiration for those who aspire to explore fields traditionally considered beyond their reach. Her story encourages individuals to follow their intellectual curiosity, irrespective of societal expectations, and to contribute meaningfully to the expansion of knowledge in diverse academic domains.

Championing Educational Equality

As we chat with Scholarly Trailblazer, we discover that her journey is not solely about personal achievement; it's about championing educational equality. In an educational landscape where gender disparities persist, she becomes an advocate for policies and initiatives that level the playing field.

Her commitment to educational equality might manifest in mentorship programs for aspiring female scholars, advocacy for inclusive curriculum development, or efforts to dismantle systemic barriers to women's educational advancement. Scholarly Trailblazer's story becomes a call to action, prompting us to actively contribute to the creation of educational environments that recognize and nurture the potential of all learners.

Balancing Education and Family

In our friendly exploration, we also uncover a significant aspect of Scholarly Trailblazer's life—the delicate balance between education and family. Navigating the demands of academia while managing familial responsibilities was an intricate dance that required resilience and support. In our conversation, she might share insights into how she negotiated this balance, the networks of support she cultivated, and the joys and challenges of harmonizing academic and familial pursuits.

Scholarly Trailblazer's story becomes a relatable narrative for many women who aspire to excel in their educational pursuits while embracing the joys of family life. Her journey encourages a reevaluation of societal expectations regarding women's roles, fostering environments that recognize and support individuals in their multifaceted pursuits.

Mentorship and Building Educational Networks

As we continue our exploration, we discover that Scholarly Trailblazer's legacy extends to mentorship and the building of educational networks. In our friendly chat, she might share stories of guiding the next generation of scholars, providing mentorship to aspiring academics, and actively working to create supportive networks within educational institutions.

Her commitment to mentorship becomes a cornerstone of her legacy—a way of paying forward the support she received and ensuring that those who come after her have guidance and encouragement on their educational journeys. Scholarly Trailblazer's story emphasizes the importance of fostering mentorship relationships and collaborative networks that uplift women in academia.

A Resilient Spirit

In the concluding pages of Scholarly Trailblazer's chapter, we encounter the resilient spirit that defines her journey. The ability to persist in the face of adversity, to rise above challenges, and to continue the pursuit of knowledge with unwavering determination becomes the heart of her story.

In our friendly dialogue, Scholarly Trailblazer might share the lessons she learned from setbacks, the moments of self-discovery that came through resilience, and the joy that accompanies the persistent pursuit of intellectual passions. Her story becomes an anthem for resilience—a reminder that the journey of education is not always smooth, but the bumps along the road are opportunities for growth and triumph.

A Call to Embrace Educational Diversity

As we bid farewell to Scholarly Trailblazer's chapter, her story extends a friendly call to embrace educational diversity. Her journey challenges us to question limiting beliefs about who belongs in academia, to actively work toward inclusivity in educational spaces, and to recognize that the pursuit of knowledge is richer when diverse voices contribute to the conversation.

Scholarly Trailblazer's legacy invites us to be advocates for educational equality, mentors to those who aspire to learn, and builders of networks that foster a supportive and inclusive academic environment. As we turn the page to our next chapter, let's carry with us the spirit of Scholarly Trailblazer—a commitment to breaking educational barriers, a passion for learning, and the understanding that, in the friendly dialogue of education, everyone has a place at the table.

61

CHAPTER 7. OVERCOMING ADVERSITY IN MEDICINE

This chapter takes us into the heart of medicine, a realm where compassion meets scientific expertise, and where women have not only practiced healing but have overcome formidable obstacles along the way. Join us in this friendly exploration of the stories of women who, against the odds, made significant contributions to the field of medicine, leaving an enduring legacy of resilience and triumph.

A Healing Calling

Let's envision our central character, whom we affectionately call Healing Pioneer, stepping into the world of medicine. In our friendly conversation with Healing Pioneer, we discover the early stirrings of her passion for healing. Born in an era when medicine was predominantly a male domain, her journey wasn't merely a career choice; it was a calling to alleviate suffering, promote health, and challenge the norms that restricted women from the medical profession.

Healing Pioneer's story emerges not just in the classrooms of medical school but in the communities she served, the patients she healed, and the challenges she faced along the way. In our friendly chat, she might share the moments of inspiration that led her to medicine, the hurdles she encountered, and the unwavering determination that propelled her forward.

Navigating the Male-Dominated Terrain

Healing Pioneer's journey unfolds against the backdrop of a male-dominated medical landscape. In an era when the notion of a woman as a physician was met with skepticism, she navigated uncharted terrain, seeking education, recognition, and acceptance within medical circles.

In our exploration, we might hear about the raised eyebrows when she entered lecture halls, the doubts she faced from colleagues, and the resilience required to prove that gender should not be a barrier to pursuing a career in medicine. Healing Pioneer's story becomes a testament to the belief that compassionate and competent medical care knows no gender.

Pioneering in Specialized Fields

As we delve deeper into Healing Pioneer's narrative, we encounter her trailblazing spirit in specialized fields of medicine. Whether she delved into surgery, research, or any other specialized area, her journey becomes a story of breaking through stereotypes and contributing to the advancement of medical knowledge.

In our friendly chat, we might explore the challenges she faced as she pursued excellence in her chosen field, the groundbreaking contributions she made, and the significance of her work in paving the way for future generations of women in specialized medical disciplines. Healing Pioneer's story becomes an inspiration for aspiring female physicians, illustrating that expertise knows no gender boundaries.

Overcoming Educational Barriers

Healing Pioneer's story is intertwined with the educational barriers she confronted. In an era when women were often excluded from medical education, she fought for admission to medical schools, sought mentorship, and pursued her studies with determination.

In our friendly conversation, we might delve into the moments when doors seemed closed, the perseverance required to gain acceptance, and the joy that accompanied each milestone achieved in her educational journey. Healing Pioneer's tale becomes a celebration of the transformative power of education and the belief that every woman should have the opportunity to pursue a career in medicine.

Providing Compassionate Care

Beyond the corridors of medical institutions, Healing Pioneer's impact is felt in the compassionate care she provided to her patients. In our exploration, we might hear stories of her bedside manner, the empathy she brought to her practice, and the relationships she cultivated with those under her care.

Her commitment to compassionate care goes beyond the medical procedures; it encompasses a holistic approach that recognizes the emotional and social dimensions of health. In our friendly chat, we might discover the joy she found in connecting with patients, the challenges of balancing scientific rigor with empathy, and the profound satisfaction derived from making a positive impact on people's lives.

Challenges in Professional Recognition

Healing Pioneer's journey is not without the challenges of professional recognition. In an environment where women were often denied the accolades and positions commensurate with their contributions, she faced obstacles in gaining promotions, obtaining leadership roles, and earning the respect of her peers.

In our friendly conversation, we might explore the moments when her accomplishments were overshadowed, the resilience required to persist in the face of professional biases, and the strategies she employed to advocate for her rightful place within the medical community. Healing Pioneer's story becomes a testament to the importance of recognizing and valuing the contributions of women in medicine.

Balancing Family and Medical Career

In the narrative of Healing Pioneer, we encounter the delicate balance between family life and a demanding medical career. Navigating the challenges of long hours, on-call duties, and the emotional toll of patient care, she found a way to harmonize her commitment to both her family and her profession.

In our friendly chat, we might delve into the support systems she cultivated, the joys and difficulties of balancing familial responsibilities, and the lessons she learned along the way. Healing Pioneer's story becomes relatable for many women who aspire to excel in their careers while cherishing the joys of family life.

Advocacy for Women in Medicine

As Healing Pioneer's narrative unfolds, we discover her commitment to advocacy for women in medicine. In our friendly conversation, she might share stories of mentorship, initiatives to address gender disparities within medical institutions, and efforts to create a more inclusive and supportive environment for female physicians.

Her advocacy work goes beyond her personal journey; it becomes a commitment to paving smoother paths for the women who will follow in her footsteps. Healing Pioneer's story becomes a call to action, encouraging the medical community to actively address gender biases, support women in their professional growth, and foster a culture of equality within the field.

Legacy in Mentorship and Medical Advancements

In the concluding pages of Healing Pioneer's chapter, we encounter the legacy she leaves through mentorship and medical advancements. In our friendly chat, she might share stories of guiding aspiring female physicians, fostering collaborative research, and contributing to medical breakthroughs that have a lasting impact on patient care.

Her commitment to mentorship becomes a source of inspiration for the next generation of women in medicine, and her contributions to medical advancements underscore the importance of diverse perspectives in driving progress. Healing Pioneer's story becomes a chapter of a broader narrative—one that recognizes the profound impact women can have on the advancement of medical science and the improvement of patient outcomes.

A Call to Dismantle Barriers in Medicine

As we bid farewell to Healing Pioneer's chapter, her story extends a friendly call to dismantle barriers in medicine. Her journey challenges us to question gender biases within the medical profession, advocate for inclusivity, and actively work toward creating environments where every aspiring physician, regardless of gender, can thrive.

Healing Pioneer's legacy encourages women to pursue careers in medicine with confidence, resilience, and a belief in their ability to make transformative contributions to the field. As we turn the page to our next chapter, let's carry with us the spirit of Healing Pioneer—a commitment to overcoming adversity, a passion for healing, and the understanding that, in the friendly dialogue of medicine, every woman has the right to be a trailblazer.

Chapter 8. Defending Human Rights

In this chapter, we embark on a journey into the realm of human rights, where the protagonists are women who have devoted their lives to defending and championing the fundamental rights of every individual. Join us in this friendly exploration of the stories of these remarkable women who, against all odds, have become tireless advocates for justice, equality, and the inherent dignity of every human being.

The Call to Justice

Picture a world where basic human rights are often trampled upon, where injustice prevails, and where the vulnerable are left without a voice. Now, imagine our central character, the Advocate of Equality, stepping into this world with a passion for justice burning in her heart. In our friendly conversation with the Advocate of Equality, we uncover the early experiences and events that ignited her commitment to defending human rights.

The Advocate of Equality's journey isn't just about legal battles; it's a compassionate response to the cries of those who suffer from oppression, discrimination, and abuse. In our friendly chat, she might share the pivotal moments that stirred her sense of justice, the mentors who guided her, and the determination that fueled her journey into the challenging yet rewarding field of human rights advocacy.

Navigating Legal Labyrinths

As we delve into the narrative of the Advocate of Equality, we find her navigating the intricate labyrinths of the legal system. In an environment where human rights violations often go unchecked, she becomes a beacon of hope for those seeking justice. In our friendly conversation, we might explore the challenges she faced in bringing human rights cases to light, the legal battles she fought, and the strategic approaches she employed to hold perpetrators accountable.

Her journey is not just about winning cases; it's about utilizing the law as a powerful tool to create systemic change. The Advocate of Equality's story becomes a testament to the belief that the legal system can be a force for good, a mechanism through which justice can be served, and a means to protect the rights of the most vulnerable in society.

Championing Gender Equality

The Advocate of Equality's commitment extends beyond generic human rights advocacy to a specific focus on gender equality. In our friendly dialogue, she might share stories of advocating for women's rights, challenging gender-based violence, and dismantling discriminatory laws and practices that perpetuate gender inequality.

Her work becomes a transformative force in societies where traditional norms often limit the rights and opportunities of women. The Advocate of Equality's story is not just about challenging legal structures but about reshaping cultural narratives and fostering environments where every individual, regardless of gender, can enjoy the full spectrum of human rights.

Protecting the Vulnerable

Human rights advocacy often involves protecting those who are most vulnerable—the marginalized, the oppressed, and those facing discrimination. In our exploration, we might hear about the Advocate of Equality's work in refugee rights, combating human trafficking, or standing up for the rights of minorities.

Her commitment to protecting the vulnerable is a reflection of the belief that the strength of a society is measured by how it treats its most marginalized members. The Advocate of Equality's story becomes a call to action, urging us all to recognize the humanity in every individual and to actively work toward creating inclusive societies that protect the rights of the most vulnerable among us.

International Advocacy

As our friendly conversation continues, we discover that the Advocate of Equality's impact transcends borders. Engaging in international advocacy, she becomes a voice for those whose rights are violated beyond the confines of a single nation. In our exploration, we might delve into her involvement in international organizations, her participation in global human rights campaigns, and her efforts to hold perpetrators accountable on the world stage.

Her work becomes a reminder that human rights are a universal concern, and defending them requires collaboration and solidarity on a global scale. The Advocate of Equality's story encourages us to think beyond national boundaries and to recognize our shared responsibility in promoting and protecting human rights worldwide.

Raising Awareness through Education

In the friendly dialogue, we uncover the Advocate of Equality's commitment to raising awareness through education. Whether through workshops, seminars, or grassroots initiatives, she actively engages in educating communities about their rights and the importance of upholding human dignity.

Her approach is not just about legal battles in courtrooms; it's about empowering individuals with knowledge and fostering a culture of rights consciousness. The Advocate of Equality's story becomes a testament to the transformative power of education as a tool for social change and human rights enlightenment.

Facing Risks with Courage

The path of human rights advocacy is not without risks, and the Advocate of Equality's story reflects moments of courage in the face of adversity. In our friendly chat, she might share experiences of threats, intimidation, or personal sacrifices made in the pursuit of justice. Yet, her unwavering commitment to the cause becomes a source of inspiration, showcasing that courage is not the absence of fear but the triumph over it.

The Advocate of Equality's journey becomes a friendly reminder that defending human rights often requires individuals to step outside their comfort zones, to confront powerful interests, and to persevere in the face of challenges. Her story encourages us to find our own reservoirs of courage, whether in advocating for others or standing up for our own rights.

Building Networks for Change

Human rights advocacy is not a solitary endeavor; it requires collaboration and the building of networks for change. In our exploration, we might uncover the Advocate of Equality's efforts in forming alliances with like-minded organizations, collaborating with grassroots activists, and leveraging the power of collective action to effect change.

Her story becomes a lesson in the importance of building bridges, fostering partnerships, and creating networks that amplify the impact of human rights advocacy. The Advocate of Equality's journey encourages us to recognize our collective strength and to actively engage in creating networks for positive change in our communities and beyond.

Legacy in Empowering Others

As we approach the conclusion of the Advocate of Equality's chapter, we encounter a pivotal theme—the legacy she leaves in empowering others. In our friendly chat, she might share stories of mentorship, of nurturing the next generation of human rights advocates, and of creating pathways for others to join the cause.

Her legacy is not measured solely by the cases she won but by the individuals she inspired to take up the mantle of human rights advocacy. The Advocate of Equality's story becomes a friendly call to empower others, to recognize the potential for change in every individual, and to actively work toward creating a world where the defense of human rights is a shared responsibility.

A Call to Action for Human Rights

As we bid farewell to the Advocate of Equality's chapter, her story extends a friendly call to action for human rights. Her journey challenges us to recognize the role each of us can play in defending the rights of others, to be advocates for justice and equality in our communities, and to actively engage in creating a world where every individual's rights are respected and protected.

The Advocate of Equality's legacy encourages us to be champions for human rights, to use our voices to speak out against injustice, and to work collaboratively to build societies that uphold the inherent dignity of every human being. As we turn the page to our next chapter, let's carry with us the inspiration of the Advocate of Equality—a commitment to defending human rights, a passion for justice, and the understanding that, in the friendly dialogue of advocacy, each of us has the power to make a difference.

CHAPTER 9. INNOVATORS IN TECHNOLOGY

In this exciting chapter, we immerse ourselves in the dynamic world of technology—a realm traditionally dominated by men. However, our protagonists, whom we fondly call Tech Pioneers, have fearlessly carved their path, leaving an indelible mark on the landscape of innovation. Join us in this friendly exploration of the stories of women who, armed with passion and determination, have transformed the tech industry, shattered stereotypes, and paved the way for future generations.

The Digital Odyssey Begins

Envision a time when the tech world echoed with the clicks of keyboards, the hum of servers, and the voices of innovators predominantly male. Now, imagine our central character, the Digital Trailblazer, stepping into this domain with a vision to reshape the future. In our friendly conversation with the Digital Trailblazer, we uncover the early days of her foray into technology—perhaps tinkering with gadgets, writing lines of code, or envisioning the endless possibilities of the digital frontier.

The Digital Trailblazer's journey is not just about mastering the intricacies of technology; it's a narrative of challenging the status quo and redefining the narrative of women in tech. In our friendly chat, she might share the moments of fascination that sparked her interest, the challenges she faced in a male-dominated industry, and the passion that fueled her journey into the exciting world of innovation.

Breaking the Silicon Ceiling

As we delve into the narrative of the Digital Trailblazer, we find her breaking through the metaphorical "Silicon Ceiling." In an industry where women were often underrepresented, she navigated the challenges of gaining recognition, accessing opportunities, and asserting her place as a tech pioneer.

In our exploration, we might hear about the stereotypes she defied, the biases she encountered, and the resilience required to ascend the ranks in a field where diversity was not always celebrated. The Digital Trailblazer's story becomes a beacon for aspiring women in technology, illustrating that the world of innovation is enriched by diverse perspectives.

Pioneering in Tech Leadership

The Digital Trailblazer's impact extends beyond coding and development—it reaches the realms of tech leadership. In our friendly conversation, we might uncover her journey to leadership positions, the strategies she employed to navigate boardrooms, and the initiatives she championed to promote diversity and inclusion within tech companies.

Her ascent to tech leadership becomes a story of not just individual achievement but of opening doors for others. The Digital Trailblazer's narrative encourages us to challenge preconceived notions about leadership in technology, emphasizing that effective leaders come in all genders and backgrounds.

Innovating for Social Impact

Our exploration with the Digital Trailblazer leads us to the innovative projects and technologies that have a broader societal impact. In our friendly chat, we might discover her ventures into developing solutions for social issues, harnessing the power of technology for positive change, and advocating for the responsible use of innovation.

Her commitment to using technology as a force for good becomes a central theme. The Digital Trailblazer's story becomes a friendly nudge for tech enthusiasts to think beyond profit margins and consider the potential of their innovations to address pressing global challenges.

Championing STEM Education

The Digital Trailblazer's journey is intertwined with a commitment to championing STEM (Science, Technology, Engineering, and Mathematics) education. In our exploration, we might hear about her efforts to inspire the next generation of tech innovators, the initiatives she supported to promote STEM education for girls, and the importance she placed on nurturing a diverse talent pool in the tech industry.

Her advocacy for STEM education becomes a pivotal aspect of her legacy. The Digital Trailblazer's story is not just about her personal achievements but about sowing the seeds for a future where young minds, regardless of gender, are empowered with the skills to drive technological innovation.

Encountering and Overcoming Tech Challenges

In our friendly dialogue with the Digital Trailblazer, we explore the challenges she encountered in the ever-evolving landscape of technology. Whether it was staying abreast of rapid advancements, overcoming industry biases, or navigating the competitive tech market, her journey becomes a friendly guide for aspiring tech professionals.

Her triumph over challenges is not just a testament to her technical prowess but also to the adaptability and resilience required in the tech industry. The Digital Trailblazer's story becomes an inspiration for individuals navigating the complexities of technology, showcasing that setbacks are stepping stones to growth and innovation.

Building Tech Communities

The Digital Trailblazer's impact extends to the communities she helped build within the tech world. In our friendly chat, we might explore her involvement in tech meetups, mentorship programs, and initiatives aimed at fostering collaboration and camaraderie within the industry.

Her commitment to building tech communities becomes a celebration of the collective power of innovation. The Digital Trailblazer's story encourages us to actively engage in tech ecosystems, share knowledge, and contribute to the creation of supportive networks that amplify the impact of individual tech pioneers.

Tech and Work-Life Integration

In our exploration, we uncover the delicate balance the Digital Trailblazer maintained between her tech career and personal life. Navigating the demands of a dynamic industry while cherishing personal relationships and pursuing passions beyond tech, she becomes a relatable figure for individuals seeking harmony between their professional and personal lives.

Her story becomes a friendly reminder that success in the tech world doesn't require sacrificing personal well-being. The Digital Trailblazer's journey encourages a holistic approach to life, where technology enhances rather than hinders the pursuit of happiness and fulfillment.

Legacy in Tech Innovation

As we approach the conclusion of the Digital Trailblazer's chapter, we encounter the legacy she leaves in tech innovation. In our friendly chat, she might share stories of groundbreaking projects, patents, or technologies that have left an enduring impact on the tech industry.

Her legacy is not merely a list of accomplishments but a narrative of contributing to the ever-evolving tapestry of technology. The Digital Trailblazer's story becomes an invitation for others to embrace innovation, push boundaries, and leave their mark on the landscape of technology.

A Call to Embrace Tech Diversity

As we bid farewell to the Digital Trailblazer's chapter, her story extends a friendly call to embrace tech diversity. Her journey challenges us to actively work toward creating inclusive tech environments, where individuals of all genders and backgrounds feel welcomed and valued.

The Digital Trailblazer's legacy encourages us to champion diversity not just for the sake of representation but for the enrichment it brings to the creative process and the potential it unlocks in the world of technology. As we turn the page to our next chapter, let's carry with us the inspiration of the Digital Trailblazer—a commitment to innovation, a passion for technology, and the understanding that, in the friendly dialogue of tech, diversity is the key to unlocking limitless possibilities.

Chapter 10. Legacy and Future Trailblazers

In this chapter, we embark on a reflective journey, celebrating the legacies of the incredible women we've encountered in the preceding chapters and looking forward with anticipation to the future trailblazers who will shape the narrative of courage, resilience, and triumph. Join us in this friendly exploration as we weave together the stories of those who have left an indelible mark and those who will carry the torch of progress into the uncharted territories that lie ahead.

Honoring Legacies

As we reflect on the stories shared in this book, we find ourselves surrounded by the rich tapestry of legacies left by remarkable women—the Scientists, Artists, Activists, Entrepreneurs, Athletes, Educators, Medical Professionals, Advocates, and Tech Pioneers. In our friendly conversation, we pay homage to the trailblazers who, through their determination, passion, and groundbreaking contributions, have paved the way for generations to come.

Their legacies are not just footprints on the sands of time but blueprints for aspiring individuals who dare to dream, challenge norms, and embark on journeys of self-discovery. In our reflections, we appreciate the courage it took for these women to stand against the tide, the resilience that fueled their pursuits, and the triumphs that became beacons of hope for others facing similar challenges.

Connecting Threads of Resilience

In our friendly exploration, we discover that the common thread weaving through each chapter is the resilient spirit of the trailblazers. Whether in science labs, art studios, boardrooms, stadiums, classrooms, clinics, courtrooms, or tech hubs, the women we've encountered displayed an unwavering resilience that transformed challenges into stepping stones.

Their stories become interconnected strands of inspiration, illustrating that resilience is not a singular trait but a dynamic force that empowers individuals to overcome adversity, learn from setbacks, and emerge stronger. As we honor their legacies, we celebrate the resilience that echoes through the pages of this book—a resilience that encourages us all to face life's challenges with fortitude and grace.

Empowering Future Trailblazers

As we reflect on the legacies of these trailblazing women, we turn our gaze toward the horizon and envision the future trailblazers yet to emerge. In our friendly conversation, we acknowledge the responsibility we bear in nurturing environments that empower individuals to become architects of change.

The stories of the trailblazers we've encountered become beacons of empowerment, urging us to create spaces where diversity is celebrated, where voices are amplified, and where individuals are encouraged to pursue their passions without fear of judgment. The legacy of these trailblazers becomes a call to action—an invitation to mentor, support, and uplift the potential trailblazers of tomorrow.

Passing the Torch

In the friendly dialogue, we acknowledge that the torch of progress is not a static flame but a dynamic beacon passed from one generation to the next. Each trailblazer, in her journey, has contributed to the illumination of this torch, and now, as we stand at the crossroads of the past and the future, we recognize the significance of passing it forward.

The legacy of the trailblazers becomes a living testament to the power of continuity—an acknowledgment that the journey toward equality, innovation, and justice is an ongoing narrative. As we pass the torch to future trailblazers, we do so with the understanding that the flame is not diminished but strengthened by the collective contributions of those who have carried it before.

Celebrating Diversity in Trailblazing

Our reflections bring us to the celebration of diversity that threads through the stories of these trailblazing women. In our friendly exploration, we recognize that diversity is not merely a checkbox but a source of strength and innovation. The trailblazers, each with a unique background, perspective, and set of experiences, have collectively shaped a narrative that transcends boundaries.

As we celebrate diversity, we embrace the idea that the tapestry of trailblazing is woven with threads of different colors, textures, and patterns. The legacy of these women becomes a testament to the beauty that emerges when diverse voices join in harmony, creating a narrative that reflects the rich complexity of the human experience.

Learning from Trailblazing Journeys

In our friendly chat, we reflect on the lessons gleaned from the trailblazing journeys chronicled in this book. The stories of courage teach us that fear is not a roadblock but a stepping stone. The narratives of resilience remind us that setbacks are not defeats but opportunities for growth. The triumphs inspire us to believe in the possibility of change, even in the face of seemingly insurmountable odds.

The trailblazing women become our mentors, offering lessons on tenacity, authenticity, and the importance of lifting others as we climb. Their journeys guide us in navigating our own paths, encouraging us to embrace challenges, celebrate victories, and remain true to our passions.

Charting Uncharted Territories

As we conclude our friendly exploration, we acknowledge that the journey of trailblazing is an ongoing adventure, with uncharted territories waiting to be explored. The legacy of the trailblazers becomes a compass, pointing toward new horizons and inviting us to venture into realms yet undiscovered.

In our reflections, we anticipate the stories of future trailblazers who will shape the narrative of courage, resilience, and triumph in ways we cannot predict. The blank pages ahead become an invitation for individuals, regardless of gender or background, to embark on their own journeys, contributing to the ever-evolving story of progress.

A Grateful Farewell

As we bid farewell to "Trailblazing Women: Stories of Courage, Resilience, and Triumph," we do so with gratitude for the friendly conversations shared, the lessons learned, and the inspiration gleaned from the remarkable women who have graced these pages. The book becomes a collective narrative, a friendly dialogue that extends beyond its chapters and into the hearts of readers.

In the spirit of the trailblazers, we carry forward the torch of progress, embracing diversity, celebrating resilience, and anticipating the stories that will shape the future. The legacy of these trailblazing women becomes a perpetual source of inspiration, inviting us to be architects of change, champions of equality, and contributors to a narrative that transcends time.

As we turn the page to new adventures, let's carry with us the friendly dialogue of "Trailblazing Women," remembering that each of us has the power to contribute to a story that celebrates courage, resilience, and triumph. The final chapter is not an endpoint but a continuum—a journey that extends beyond these pages and into the uncharted territories of tomorrow.

Navigating the Trial of Triumph

Dear Reader,

As we reach the conclusion of "Trailblazing Women: Stories of Courage, Resilience, and Triumph," we stand at the crossroads of inspiration and reflection. This book has been a journey—a journey through the narratives of extraordinary women who, against the backdrop of societal norms and expectations, dared to forge paths of their own. Their stories, woven together in these pages, form a tapestry that celebrates not only individual triumphs but the collective spirit of resilience and courage that defines the trailblazing journey.

In our exploration, we've ventured into the realms of science, arts, activism, entrepreneurship, sports, education, medicine, advocacy, and technology. Each chapter has unfolded a new dimension of the trailblazing narrative, introducing us to women who defied expectations, shattered barriers, and left an indelible mark on their respective fields. Their stories, infused with passion and determination, echo the sentiment that the trail of triumph is navigated not by the faint of heart but by those who embrace challenges as opportunities and setbacks as stepping stones.

Themes of Courage

Throughout our friendly conversations with the Scholars, Pioneers, Artists, Advocates, and Tech Pioneers, a recurring theme has been courage. Whether it was the courage to challenge societal norms, pursue education against the odds, pioneer innovations in male-dominated fields, or advocate for justice and equality, these women exemplify the essence of courage. Their stories invite us to reconsider our own definitions of bravery—to see courage not as the absence of fear but as the audacity to dream, the resolve to face challenges head-on, and the determination to persevere in the pursuit of one's passion.

Threads of Resilience

Resilience, a golden thread woven into the fabric of each chapter, emerges as a guiding principle in the trailblazing journey. From overcoming adversities in education and navigating bias in professional settings to pushing the boundaries of technological innovation, the trailblazers have showcased a resilience that transforms challenges into catalysts for growth. Their narratives become a source of inspiration for anyone facing obstacles, reminding us that resilience is not only a survival skill but a transformative force that propels individuals toward greater heights.

Triumphs Across Fields

The triumphs chronicled in these pages are as diverse as the fields themselves. In science, we've witnessed groundbreaking discoveries and contributions that redefine our understanding of the world. In the arts, we've marveled at the creativity that transcends boundaries and challenges societal norms. In entrepreneurship, we've celebrated the establishment of successful ventures that defy gender stereotypes. In sports, we've cheered for athletes who've not only excelled in their fields but shattered glass ceilings. In education, we've explored the transformative power of knowledge and the commitment to inclusive learning environments. In medicine, we've been inspired by stories of healing and advocacy for equitable healthcare. In activism, we've stood alongside women defending human rights and championing justice. In business and technology, we've witnessed the reshaping of industries and the championing of diversity. Each triumph is a testament to the potential for change, the possibility of rewriting narratives, and the enduring spirit of trailblazers.

Celebrating Diversity

Diversity emerges as a central theme, not just in terms of gender but in the breadth of experiences, backgrounds, and perspectives that these trailblazers bring to their respective fields. The richness of the narrative lies in the celebration of this diversity—an acknowledgment that progress is propelled by the fusion of different voices, ideas, and experiences. The book becomes a testament to the power of inclusion, encouraging us to foster environments that embrace diversity as a catalyst for innovation and growth.

The Intersectionality of Trailblazing

As we conclude our exploration, it is essential to acknowledge the intersectionality inherent in the trailblazing journeys. The experiences of these women are shaped not only by their gender but also by factors such as race, ethnicity, socioeconomic background, and more. The intersectionality of their stories calls for a nuanced understanding of the challenges faced by individuals who navigate multiple layers of identity. It prompts us to engage in conversations that go beyond gender, recognizing the interconnected nature of societal structures and the importance of addressing issues with an inclusive lens.

The Legacy Left Behind

The legacy left behind by the trailblazers is a legacy of inspiration, empowerment, and possibility. Their stories ripple through time, inviting us to reflect on our own capacities for courage, resilience, and triumph. The scholars, artists, entrepreneurs, athletes, educators, medical professionals, advocates, and tech pioneers become beacons, illuminating the path for those who will follow. Their legacies extend beyond individual achievements, becoming a collective narrative that contributes to the ongoing story of progress.

The Torch Passed Forward

In the spirit of the trailblazers, the torch of progress is passed forward. The book is not a conclusion but a continuation—an invitation for readers to engage with the narratives, to find resonance in the stories, and to contribute to the ongoing dialogue of empowerment and equality. The journey does not end with the turning of the last page; rather, it extends into the choices we make, the conversations we have, and the actions we take in our own lives and communities.

A Friendly Invitation

As we bid farewell to the trailblazing women who have graced these pages, we extend a friendly invitation to you, dear reader. Let their stories be catalysts for conversations, sparks for new ideas, and inspiration for your own journey. Engage in friendly dialogues that challenge stereotypes, celebrate diversity, and foster environments where everyone, regardless of gender, has the opportunity to blaze their trail.

In the spirit of camaraderie, let's carry forward the lessons learned, the inspiration gained, and the torch of progress. May the trailblazing spirit embedded in these pages continue to ignite curiosity, fuel resilience, and inspire triumphs—both big and small. As we navigate our own trails, may we do so with the courage to challenge norms, the resilience to face setbacks, and the triumphs that come from embracing our authentic selves.

Thank you for joining us on this trail of triumph. May your own journey be filled with courage, resilience, and triumph as you navigate the paths that lie ahead.

"As we close this chapter of 'Trailblazing Women,' let the echoes of their courage inspire us, the resilience of their journeys guide us, and the triumphs of their stories propel us forward, ever onward in the pursuit of a world where every individual can blaze their unique and unbounded trail."

Milton Keynes UK
Ingram Content Group UK Ltd.
UKHW020049181024
449757UK00011B/576